A Better Thing to Do

The Story of Jesus and Mary and Martha

We are grateful to the following team of authors for their contributions to *God Loves Me,* a Bible story program for young children. This Bible story, one of a series of fifty-two, was written by Patricia L. Nederveld, managing editor for CRC Publications. Suggestions for using this book were developed by Jesslyn DeBoer, a freelance author from Grand Rapids, Michigan. Yvonne Van Ee, an early childhood educator, served as project consultant and wrote *God Loves Me,* the program guide that accompanies this series of Bible storybooks.

Nederveld has served as a consultant to Title I early childhood programs in Colorado. She has extensive experience as a writer, teacher, and consultant for federally funded preschool, kindergarten, and early childhood programs in Colorado, Texas, Michigan, Florida, Missouri, and Washington, using the *High/Scope* Education Research Foundation curriculum. In addition to writing the *Bible Footprints* church curriculum for four- and five-year-olds, Nederveld edited the revised *Threes* curriculum and the first edition of preschool through second grade materials for the *LiFE* curriculum, all published by CRC Publications.

DeBoer has served as a church preschool leader and as coauthor of the preschool-kindergarten materials for the *LiFE* curriculum published by CRC Publications. She has also written K-6 science and health curriculum for Christian Schools International and gift books for the Zondervan Corporation, Grand Rapids, Michigan.

Van Ee is a professor and early childhood program advisor in the Education Department at Calvin College, Grand Rapids, Michigan. She has served as curriculum author and consultant for Christian Schools International and wrote the original *Story Hour* organization manual and curriculum materials for fours and fives.

Photo on page 5: Sue Ann Miller/Tony Stone Images; photo on page 20: Rosanne Olson/Tony Stone Images.

Library of Congress Cataloging-in-Publication Data

Nederveld, Patricia L., 1944-
    A better thing to do: the story of Jesus and Mary and Martha/Patricia L. Nederveld.
        p. cm. — (God loves me; bk. 38)
    Summary: Retells the Bible story of two very different sisters and what they
learned when Jesus visited their home. Includes follow-up activities.
        ISBN 1-56212-307-6
    1. Mary, of Bethany, Saint—Juvenile literature. 2. Martha, Saint
—Juvenile literature. 3. Bible stories, English—N.T. Luke
[1. Mary, of Bethany, Saint. 2. Martha, Saint. 3. Bible stories—N.T.]
I. Title. II. Series: Nederveld, Patricia L., 1944- God loves me; bk. 38.
BS2490.M2N43   1998
232.9'5—dc21   98-16965
                                                                   CIP
                                                                   AC

10 9 8 7 6 5 4 3 2 1

A Better Thing to Do

The Story of Jesus and Mary and Martha

PATRICIA L. NEDERVELD

ILLUSTRATIONS BY PATRICK KELLEY

CRC Publications
Grand Rapids, Michigan

This is a story from God's book, the Bible.

It's for <small>say name(s) of your child(ren).</small>
It's for me too!

Luke 10:38-42

Make the beds,
clean the house—
sweep the dirty floor.
Martha's getting ready—
is that Jesus at the door?

Shop for
groceries,
bake the
bread—
set the table too.
Martha's getting
ready—
Jesus, is that you?

Martha's sister, Mary, is getting ready too.
When Jesus comes to visit she knows just what she'll do.

Listening to Jesus
is what Mary
wants to do.
He tells her such
amazing things,
things she never
knew!

15

S ister Martha's
getting
angry—
"Why, this just
isn't fair!
Tell Mary she must
help me!"
says Martha with
a glare.

" Martha,
you're too
busy.
You're feeling
worried too.
But Mary wants to
listen—
that's a better
thing to do!"

I wonder if you know that Jesus is happy when we listen to stories from the Bible . . .

Dear God, thank you for the stories in the Bible. We want to be good listeners like Mary. Amen.

Suggestions for Follow-up

Opening

Bring an assortment of the Bible storybooks from the *God Loves Me* series. Encourage the children to look through the books as they arrive today. Do they remember any of the stories you've read together? Invite them to retell the story in their own words as they look at the pictures.

When you gather your group to hear today's story, show the children a Bible. Tell them that the Bible has many stories about God's love. As you talk, slowly flip through the pages. Tell the children that when they listen to stories from the Bible, they are listening to God. God talks to us in the Bible. Begin reading this storybook at page 4. As you read page 4, gently touch each child and say the child's name.

Learning Through Play

Learning through play is the best way! The following activity suggestions are meant to help you provide props and experiences that will invite the children to play their way into the Scripture story and its simple truth. Try to provide plenty of time for the children to choose their own activities and to play individually. Use group activities sparingly—little ones learn most comfortably with a minimum of structure.

1. As the children build with blocks, encourage them to build a church where people can come to hear Bible stories. Or invite them to pretend to read a Bible story to their family of dolls or stuffed animals as they play house. Remind them that Mary sat quietly and listened to Jesus tell about God's love. We can listen too!

2. Provide simple dress-up clothes and props, and invite your little ones to act out the roles of Mary and Martha. Let children pretend to do all the things Martha was doing in the story. Help your little ones sense that we all need to find quiet time, and encourage them to listen to God's Word like Mary did. Read the story again or another favorite story, and quietly sing or hum "Jesus Loves Me" (Songs Section, *God Loves Me* program guide) as children enjoy this time of listening.

3. Provide materials in your art area the children can use to make a bookmark for their family's Bible or story Bible. Make copies of the bookmark (see Pattern P, Patterns Section, *God Loves Me* program guide) on brightly colored cardstock, and cut them out. Set out heart and Bible stickers, and invite your little ones to decorate back of the bookmark. Write each child's name in the blank space. If you wish, punch a hole in the top, and add a yarn tassle you've prepared ahead of time. Show the children how to mark a page in your Bible or storybook. Remind them that Jesus is happy when we listen to stories from the Bible.

4. Sing or say the words from the song "Two Little Eyes" (Songs Section, *God Loves Me* program guide) as your little ones follow your actions:

Two little eyes to look to God, (point to each
eye; point up)
two little ears to hear his Word, (point to each
ear)
two little feet to walk his ways, (point to feet;
step in place)
hands to serve God all my days. (put hands
out, palms up)
　　　—Words: anonymous

5. Visit your church library during your time
together today. Arrange ahead of time for
someone to assist you with checking out books.
Invite your little ones to select one book to
borrow for the week. If you don't have a
church library, you may want to provide a
collection of Bible storybooks (like the *God
Loves Me* series) that children could borrow.
Send a note to parents requesting them to
return the books the following week. Express
your joy that each child will have a story from
God's Word to listen to at home.

Closing

Draw your group around you, and sit quietly for a
moment. Then, almost in a whisper, say the prayer
on page 21.

At Home

Make daily Bible reading an important part of
your child's life by integrating the habit with
some other daily routine such as mealtime or
bedtime. You may want to keep a favorite Bible
storybook or a set of Bible storybooks in a
special place in your kitchen or in your child's
room. Since children love to hear the same
story over and over, you may want to try new
ways to enjoy the story together. Look at the
pictures, and ask your little one to describe
what the characters are doing or what feelings
they must have. Have your child "read" the
story to you. Or for fun, make exaggerated
mistakes as you read the story, and let your
little one correct your reading. These shared
times around God's Word can build memories
of close times together.

Old Testament Stories

Blue and Green and Purple Too! *The Story of God's Colorful World*

It's a Noisy Place! *The Story of the First Creatures*

Adam and Eve *The Story of the First Man and Woman*

Take Good Care of My World! *The Story of Adam and Eve in the Garden*

A Very Sad Day *The Story of Adam and Eve's Disobedience*

A Rainy, Rainy Day *The Story of Noah*

Count the Stars! *The Story of God's Promise to Abraham and Sarah*

A Girl Named Rebekah *The Story of God's Answer to Abraham*

Two Coats for Joseph *The Story of Young Joseph*

Plenty to Eat *The Story of Joseph and His Brothers*

Safe in a Basket *The Story of Baby Moses*

I'll Do It! *The Story of Moses and the Burning Bush*

Safe at Last! *The Story of Moses and the Red Sea*

What Is It? *The Story of Manna in the Desert*

A Tall Wall *The Story of Jericho*

A Baby for Hannah *The Story of an Answered Prayer*

Samuel! Samuel! *The Story of God's Call to Samuel*

Lions and Bears! *The Story of David the Shepherd Boy*

David and the Giant *The Story of David and Goliath*

A Little Jar of Oil *The Story of Elisha and the Widow*

One, Two, Three, Four, Five, Six, Seven! *The Story of Elisha and Naaman*

A Big Fish Story *The Story of Jonah*

Lions, Lions! *The Story of Daniel*

New Testament Stories

Jesus Is Born! *The Story of Christmas*

Good News! *The Story of the Shepherds*

An Amazing Star! *The Story of the Wise Men*

Waiting, Waiting, Waiting! *The Story of Simeon and Anna*

Who Is This Child? *The Story of Jesus in the Temple*

Follow Me! *The Story of Jesus and His Twelve Helpers*

The Greatest Gift *The Story of Jesus and the Woman at the Well*

A Father's Wish *The Story of Jesus and a Little Boy*

Just Believe! *The Story of Jesus and a Little Girl*

Get Up and Walk! *The Story of Jesus and a Man Who Couldn't Walk*

A Little Lunch *The Story of Jesus and a Hungry Crowd*

A Scary Storm *The Story of Jesus and a Stormy Sea*

Thank You, Jesus! *The Story of Jesus and One Thankful Man*

A Wonderful Sight! *The Story of Jesus and a Man Who Couldn't See*

A Better Thing to Do *The Story of Jesus and Mary and Martha*

A Lost Lamb *The Story of the Good Shepherd*

Come to Me! *The Story of Jesus and the Children*

Have a Great Day! *The Story of Jesus and Zacchaeus*

I Love You, Jesus! *The Story of Mary's Gift to Jesus*

Hosanna! *The Story of Palm Sunday*

The Best Day Ever! *The Story of Easter*

Goodbye—for Now *The Story of Jesus' Return to Heaven*

A Prayer for Peter *The Story of Peter in Prison*

Sad Day, Happy Day! *The Story of Peter and Dorcas*

A New Friend *The Story of Paul's Conversion*

Over the Wall *The Story of Paul's Escape in a Basket*

A Song in the Night *The Story of Paul and Silas in Prison*

A Ride in the Night *The Story of Paul's Escape on Horseback*

The Shipwreck *The Story of Paul's Rescue at Sea*

Holiday Stories

Selected stories from the New Testament to help you celebrate the Christian year

Jesus Is Born! *The Story of Christmas*

Good News! *The Story of the Shepherds*

An Amazing Star! *The Story of the Wise Men*

Hosanna! *The Story of Palm Sunday*

The Best Day Ever! *The Story of Easter*

Goodbye—for Now *The Story of Jesus' Return to Heaven*

These fifty-two books are the heart of *God Loves Me*, a Bible story program designed for young children. Individual books (or the entire set) and the accompanying program guide *God Loves Me* are available from CRC Publications (1-800-333-8300).